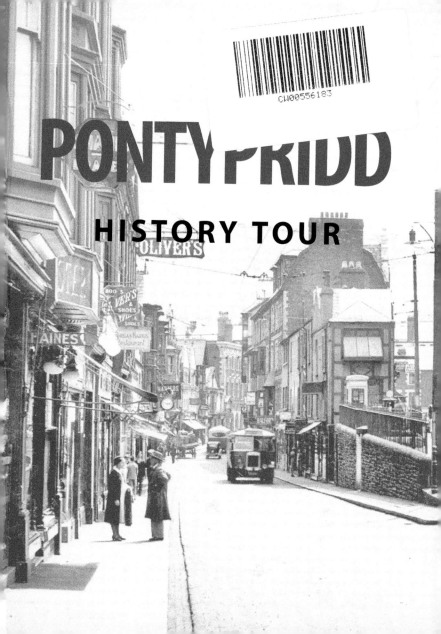

PONTYPRIDD

HISTORY TOUR

First published 2011
This edition published 2014

Amberley Publishing
The Hill, Stroud,
Gloucestershire, GL5 4EP
www.amberley-books.com

Copyright © Alun Seward & David
Swidenbank, 2014

The right of Alun Seward & David
Swidenbank to be identified as the
Author of this work has been asserted in
accordance with the Copyrights, Designs
and Patents Act 1988.

ISBN 978 1 4456 4150 8 (print)
ISBN 978 1 4456 4164 5 (ebook)

British Library Cataloguing in
Publication Data.
A catalogue record for this book is
available from the British Library.

Typesetting by Amberley Publishing.
Printed in Great Britain.

Map on pages 6 & 7 courtesy of
OS Streetview

INTRODUCTION

Pontypridd was not always so called; this usage dates only from 1856. Its prior name, an English one, was Newbridge. Today's title derives, according to the majority of sources, from a shortening of the literal Welsh – Pont-y-Ty-Pridd (Bridge of the Earthen House). The single-span, stone bridge over the Taff, regarded around the world as 'Bridge of Beauty', was constructed in 1755 by William Edwards. A proud link to the town's origins, it still stands today alongside a later addition.

This iconic South Wales town ('Ponty' in its famous short form) lies in the lee of close mountainous masses that rise precipitously to some 1,250 feet, squeezing the landscape tightly at this convergence of three valleys.

The new transport requirements of the Industrial Revolution in metals and mining capitalised upon the small settlement's convenient river crossing on the old drovers' route from the South Wales coastline to Merthyr and the hill country. The changes began at Treforest, where the grasp of local geography relaxed into wider contours and the Taff flowed less fiercely. However, quicker and better bridge building and the advent of the Glamorganshire Canal soon empowered Pontypridd's dominance.

The town's formation and rapid growth transformed Taff Vale's peaceful, pastoral meadows at the confluence of the rivers Rhondda and Taff into an industrial conduit.

It became the sentinel access way to transport the riches extracted from the deep, carboniferous cloisters of the Rhondda, Cynon and Clydach valleys to city and ports. Increasing volumes of coal soon necessitated the construction of the Taff Vale Railway. Pontypridd's station became the hub of the valleys' industrial fortune; its platforms were considered the longest of any railway at the time.

New shops and services opened in Taff and Mill Streets to service the requirements of the exploding populations of satellite mining villages, and chapels and churches rapidly clustered around the bustling central markets; the prosperous town was firmly 'on the map'.

But from these high points, the post-Second World War era saw a steady, irreversible decline of 'King Coal', mirrored by the faltering fortunes of the town. The author remembers it still vibrant in the 1950s, before 1960s cuts decimated Ponty's railway tracks, undermining the town's endeavours. The final pit closure at Lady Windsor in 1988 was a resounding blow to local prosperity.

Nevertheless, Pontypridd's iconic identity, along with its knack for producing precocious talent in all fields of public endeavour, has enabled its survival. In that same year, the town opened European links by twinning with Nurtingen in Southern Germany – the first such link in Rhondda-Cynon-Taff's history.

Today, the town's population approaches 3,000, while Pontypridd's larger community is home to over 29,000 folk.

The area still evidences a cross-section of high-achieving institutions. The enduring Treforest Industrial Estate, plus its smaller satellites encouraged onto previous pit lands, provides diverse employment, along with retail warehousing. In education, there are English- and Welsh-medium schools, and the strong growth of the young University of Glamorgan's campus. One of the largest relief highway schemes in Europe now eases local access to the M4 and A470 trunk routes for a burgeoning, increasingly prosperous, commuting catchment.

David and I are delighted to have revisited so many of the places I experienced as a boy, when I would buy Saturday 'away-day' rail returns from Treorchy at 9 old pence and run along that longest platform. I would visit bustling shops, the market with its bewildering array of scents and colours, and the mystical, steamy cafés of the 'Italian' connection.

Today, Ponty still delights, especially the green lung of the 'People's Park', its listed Lido soon to be restored. Optimistic improvements have also seen a new riverside commercial development open in 2012 and the town's persona revitalised by a £10 million 'street-scape' face-lift. Imposing public buildings sit alongside sensitive heritage preservations and revived buildings. Favourite older shops and venues are joined by chain stores; innovative businesses include the likes of a high-class delicatessen, a brasserie, a boutique hotel, and a young, award-winning brewery.

To borrow from a hit song from Sir Tom Jones (though from Treforest, considered one of Ponty's famous sons, who's come from Mr via 'Squire' and 'Senator', to become a Knight of the Realm!) – the grass of home is still green.

Despite its trials – on which the jury is still out – Pontypridd lives! Long may it be so.

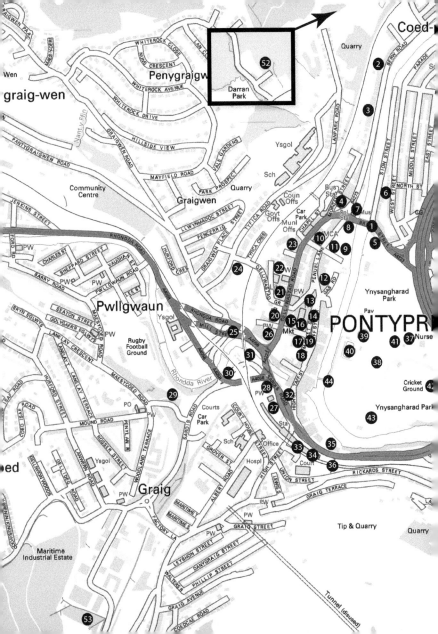

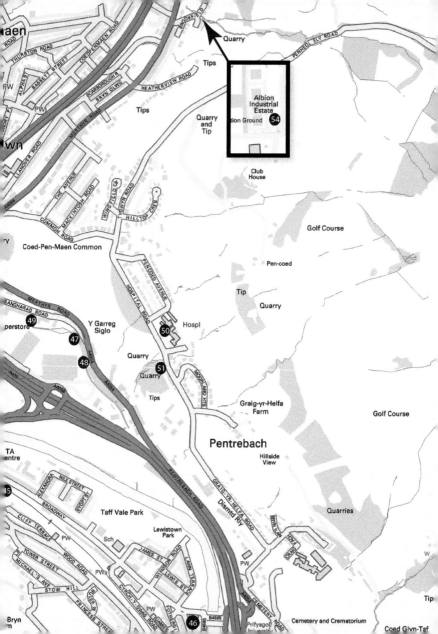

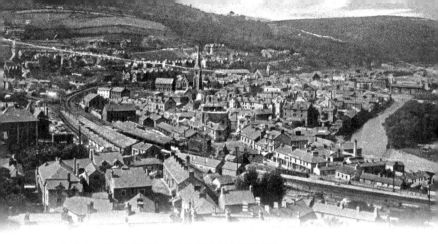

PONTYPRIDD TOWNSHIP

Viewed from the vantage of its southern heights, the town is dominated by the natural amphitheatre of mountains. The rivers Taff and Rhondda carve through the area's stone layers to their confluence. This view crystallises the changes: the bold A470 dual carriageway hugs the eastern escarpment to pass close by the town on high, concrete stilts – part of a motoring clearway from Cardiff, running north to Merthyr.

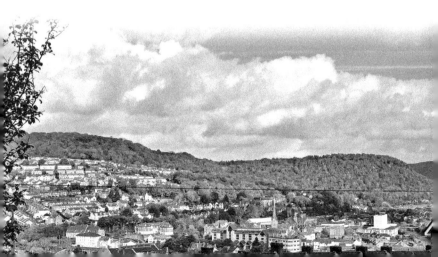

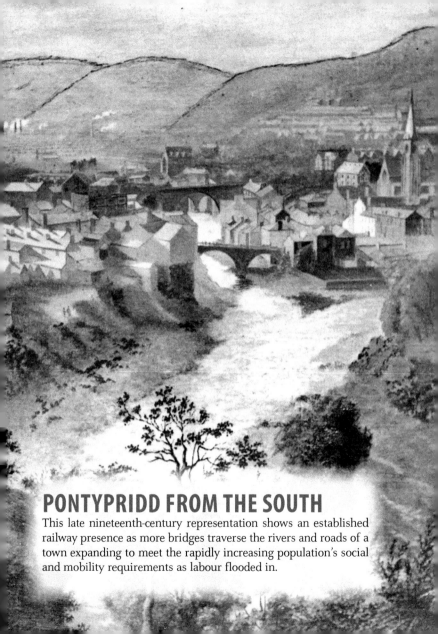

PONTYPRIDD FROM THE SOUTH

This late nineteenth-century representation shows an established railway presence as more bridges traverse the rivers and roads of a town expanding to meet the rapidly increasing population's social and mobility requirements as labour flooded in.

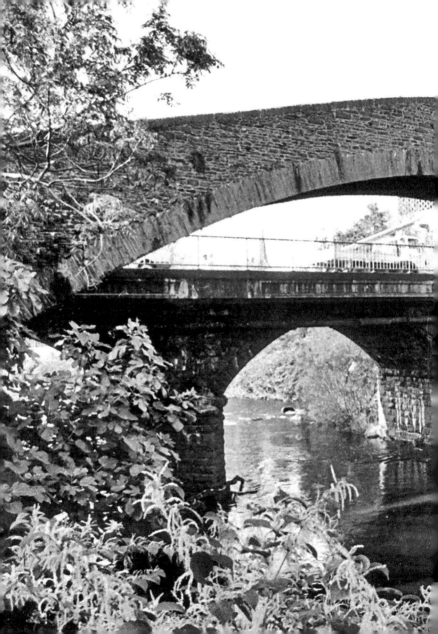

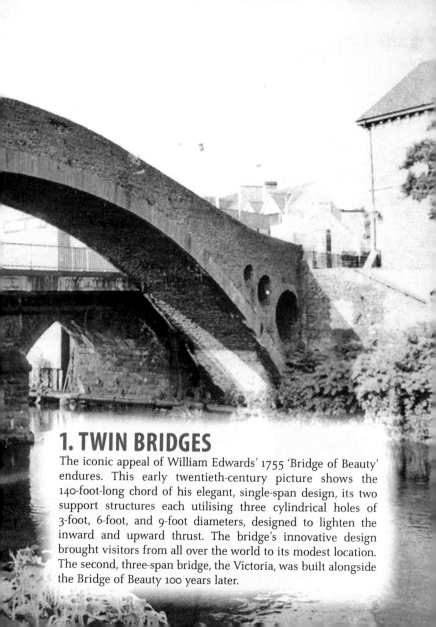

1. TWIN BRIDGES

The iconic appeal of William Edwards' 1755 'Bridge of Beauty' endures. This early twentieth-century picture shows the 140-foot-long chord of his elegant, single-span design, its two support structures each utilising three cylindrical holes of 3-foot, 6-foot, and 9-foot diameters, designed to lighten the inward and upward thrust. The bridge's innovative design brought visitors from all over the world to its modest location. The second, three-span bridge, the Victoria, was built alongside the Bridge of Beauty 100 years later.

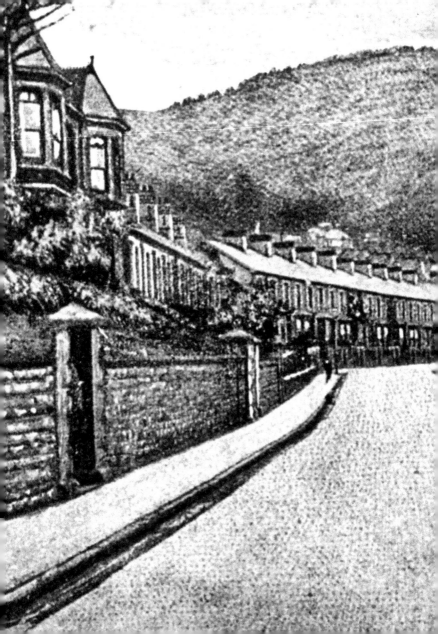

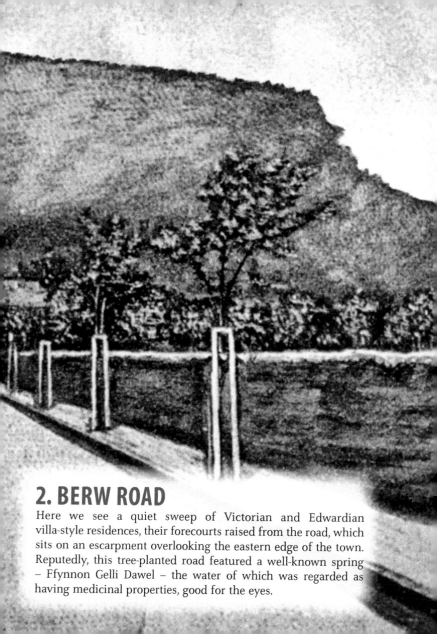

2. BERW ROAD

Here we see a quiet sweep of Victorian and Edwardian villa-style residences, their forecourts raised from the road, which sits on an escarpment overlooking the eastern edge of the town. Reputedly, this tree-planted road featured a well-known spring – Ffynnon Gelli Dawel – the water of which was regarded as having medicinal properties, good for the eyes.

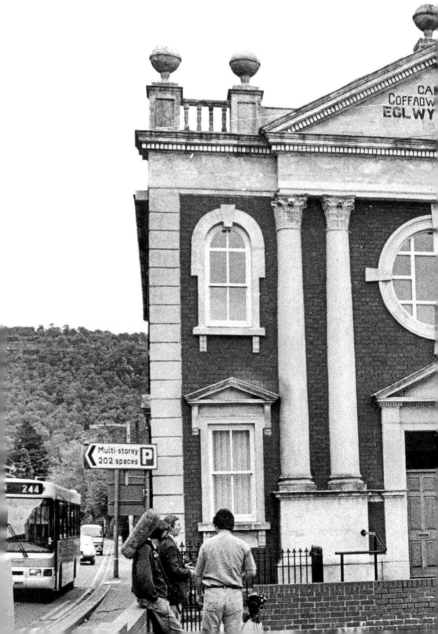

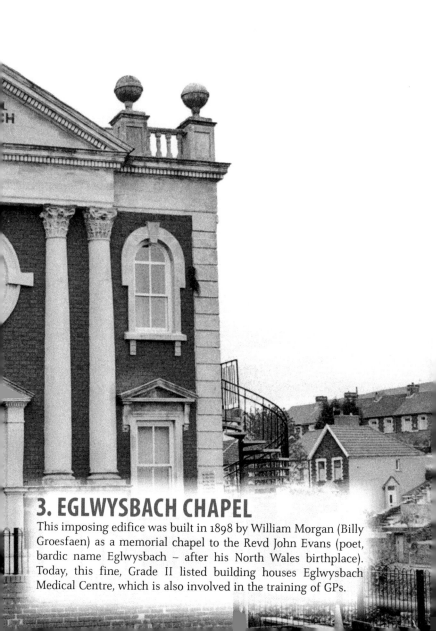

3. EGLWYSBACH CHAPEL

This imposing edifice was built in 1898 by William Morgan (Billy Groesfaen) as a memorial chapel to the Revd John Evans (poet, bardic name Eglwysbach – after his North Wales birthplace). Today, this fine, Grade II listed building houses Eglwysbach Medical Centre, which is also involved in the training of GPs.

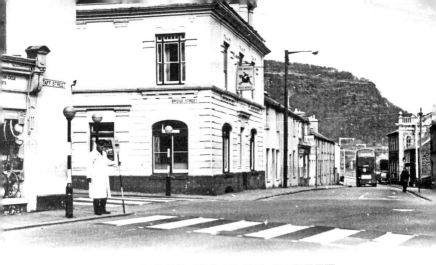

4. BERW ROAD/BRIDGE STREET

Bridge Street as it continued east, with the Hancock's Ely Brewery fuelled Bridge Hotel an imposing corner presence from yesteryear. The Taff Street zebra crossing attended by a lollipop man was soon to change form again. Today, the substantial terrace, including the hotel, has been demolished for the 1960s redevelopment of the new police station and its integral car park site.

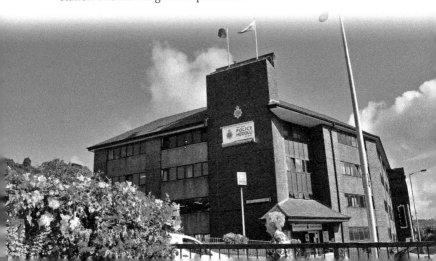

5. BRIDGE STREET

This early watercolour, signed by P. Dabell, of John and Ida's parkside café premises, shows its smart frontage details indicating its establishment in the year of the coronation of HM Queen Elizabeth II.

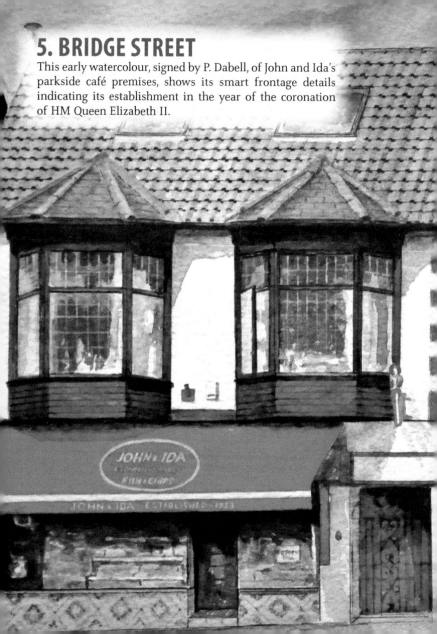

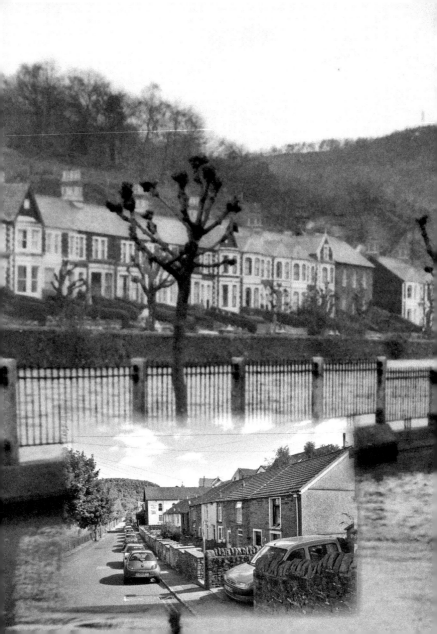

6. SION STREET

The turbulent waters of the Taff, swollen by mountain run-offs and tributaries, washed debris downstream, which caught at the first bridges to dam and flood the riverside Sion Street, as the dramatic early picture shows. Today, after restoration work, the strong, low-lying terrace sits behind a protective walled bankside, and has recovered its edge-of-town poise.

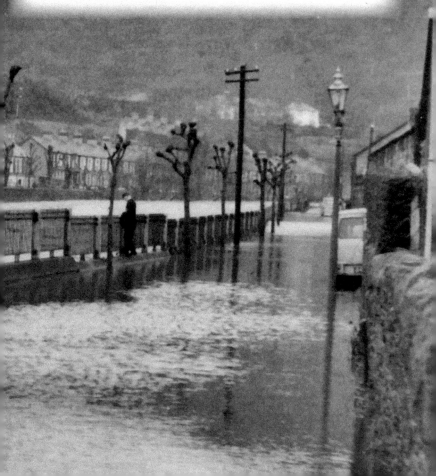

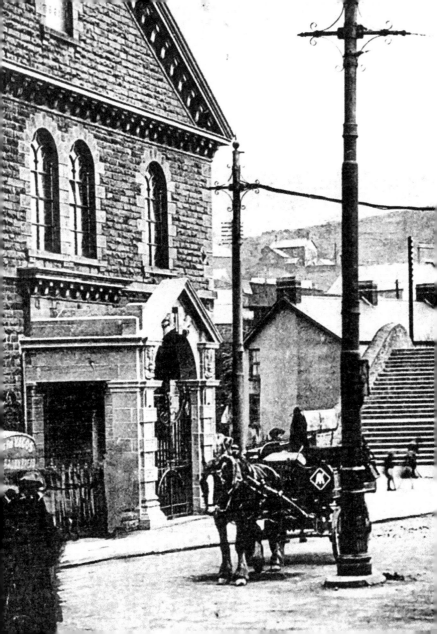

7. TABERNACLE CHAPEL

This imposing Welsh Independent chapel was built in 1861 and refurbished 1910. This small chapel provided English-language worship. Today, the identity of this chapel, alongside the iconic town bridge, has changed, and it is dedicated to the preservation of the town's history as a fine historical centre, museum and ground-floor gallery. A retained feature of its previous incarnation is the magnificent organ inset to an elegant, arched alcove, which complements the fine, ornate interior. It is worth a visit.

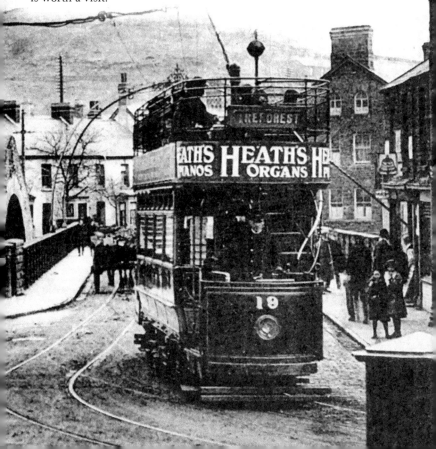

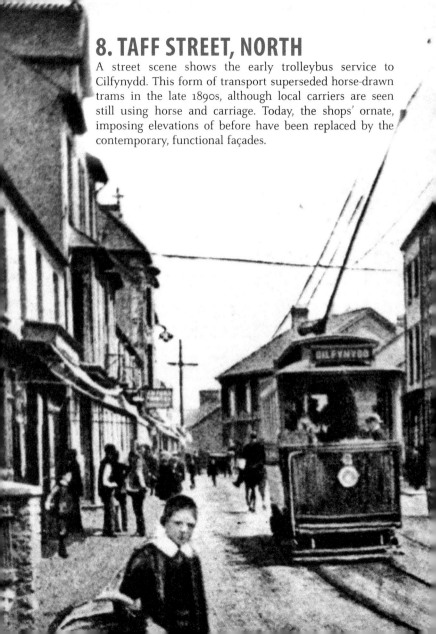

8. TAFF STREET, NORTH

A street scene shows the early trolleybus service to Cilfynydd. This form of transport superseded horse-drawn trams in the late 1890s, although local carriers are seen still using horse and carriage. Today, the shops' ornate, imposing elevations of before have been replaced by the contemporary, functional façades.

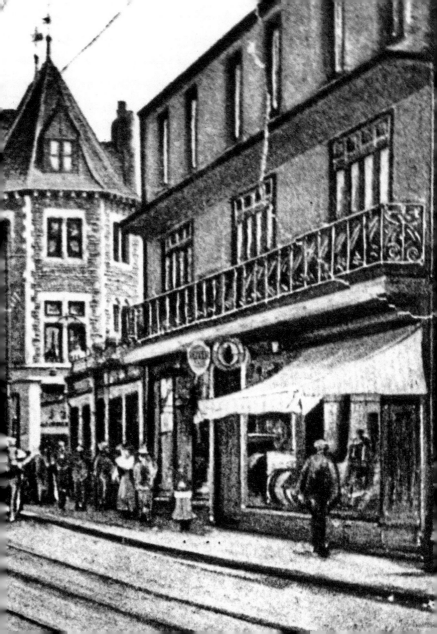

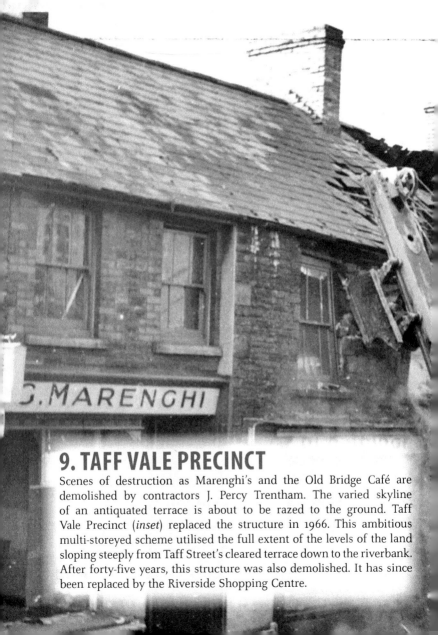

G.MARENGHI

9. TAFF VALE PRECINCT

Scenes of destruction as Marenghi's and the Old Bridge Café are demolished by contractors J. Percy Trentham. The varied skyline of an antiquated terrace is about to be razed to the ground. Taff Vale Precinct (*inset*) replaced the structure in 1966. This ambitious multi-storeyed scheme utilised the full extent of the levels of the land sloping steeply from Taff Street's cleared terrace down to the riverbank. After forty-five years, this structure was also demolished. It has since been replaced by the Riverside Shopping Centre.

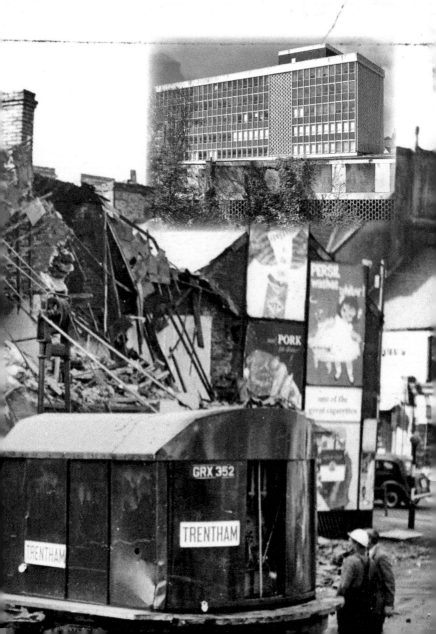

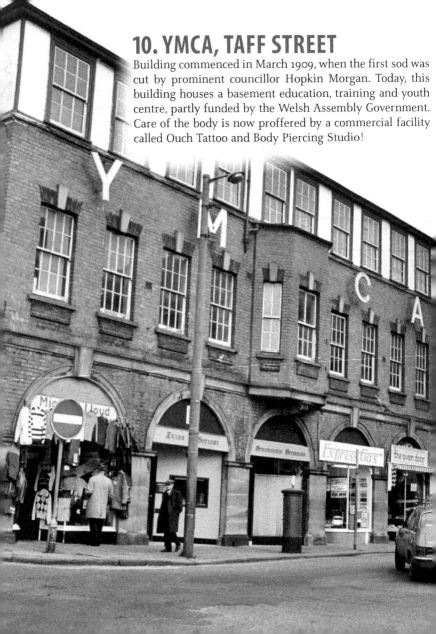

10. YMCA, TAFF STREET

Building commenced in March 1909, when the first sod was cut by prominent councillor Hopkin Morgan. Today, this building houses a basement education, training and youth centre, partly funded by the Welsh Assembly Government. Care of the body is now proffered by a commercial facility called Ouch Tattoo and Body Piercing Studio!

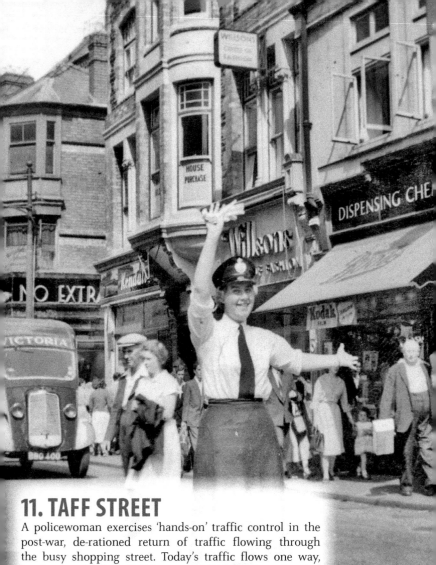

11. TAFF STREET

A policewoman exercises 'hands-on' traffic control in the post-war, de-rationed return of traffic flowing through the busy shopping street. Today's traffic flows one way, north to south, along Taff Street, which is mainly pedestrian access, with only buses and taxis, and is policed by an innovative remote-controlled system of inset bollards.

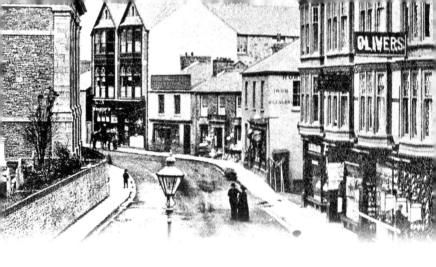

12. TAFF STREET

To the left-hand side is the wall of Penuel chapel's forecourt; the graves within were soon to be removed. Opposite, at the premises of Olivers Shoes, sign-hangers can be seen working on the shop's frontage. Today, the large former frontages are developed to accommodate more shops. The building immediately after the small lane break has been demolished, enabling a wider access to the rear public car park.

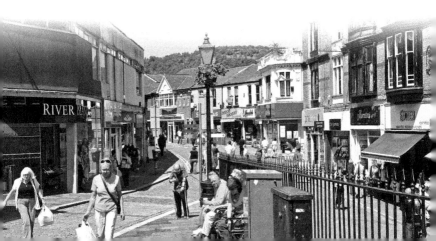

13. PENUEL SQUARE

This elegant stone fountain was donated by Sir Alfred Thomas, MP, later Lord Pontypridd, to supply fresh drinking water to passers-by and animals. The structure features a pinnacle of two dragons supporting a lit globe. Today, Penuel Square still features the historic fountain, now relocated to a lower grounding and overlooked by a modern commercial parade.

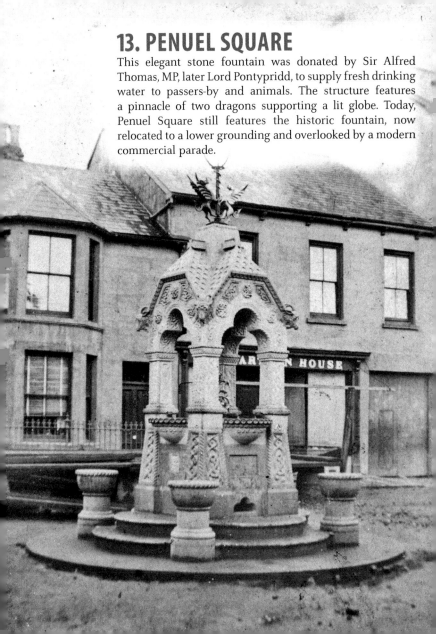

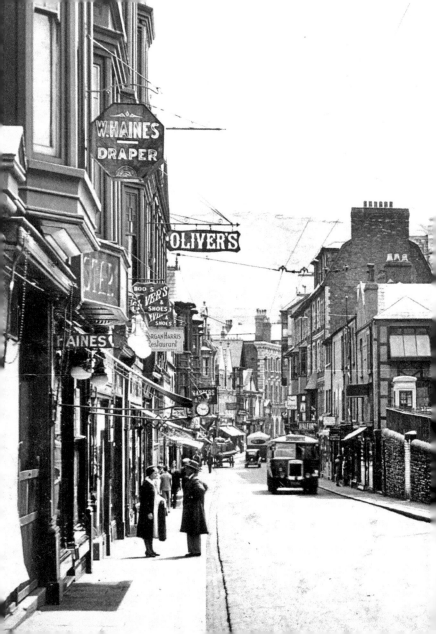

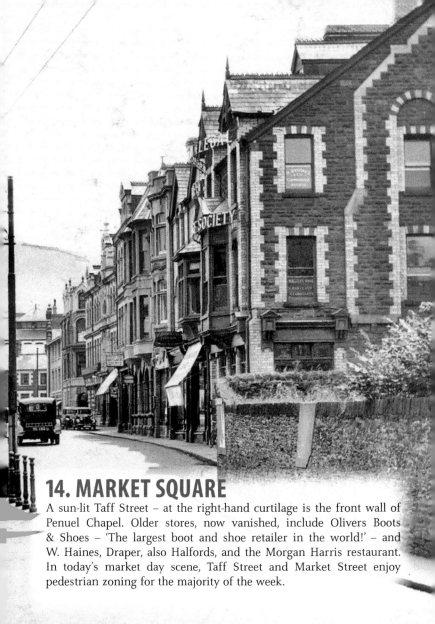

14. MARKET SQUARE

A sun-lit Taff Street – at the right-hand curtilage is the front wall of Penuel Chapel. Older stores, now vanished, include Olivers Boots & Shoes – 'The largest boot and shoe retailer in the world!' – and W. Haines, Draper, also Halfords, and the Morgan Harris restaurant. In today's market day scene, Taff Street and Market Street enjoy pedestrian zoning for the majority of the week.

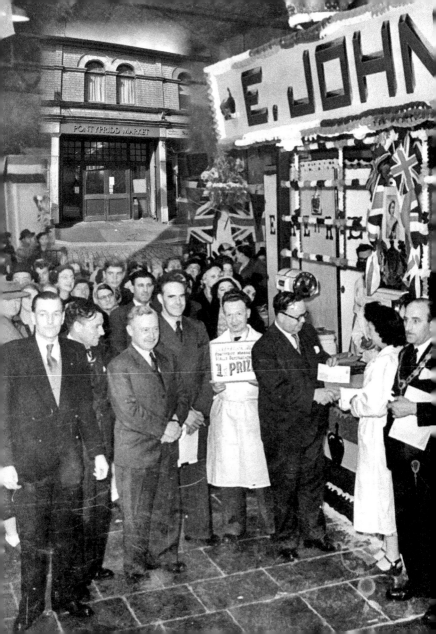

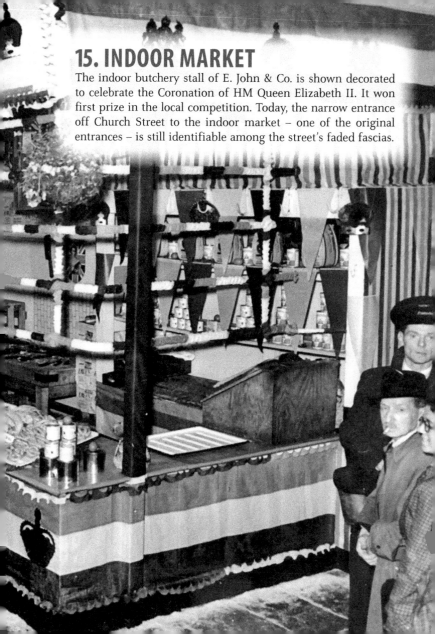

15. INDOOR MARKET

The indoor butchery stall of E. John & Co. is shown decorated to celebrate the Coronation of HM Queen Elizabeth II. It won first prize in the local competition. Today, the narrow entrance off Church Street to the indoor market – one of the original entrances – is still identifiable among the street's faded fascias.

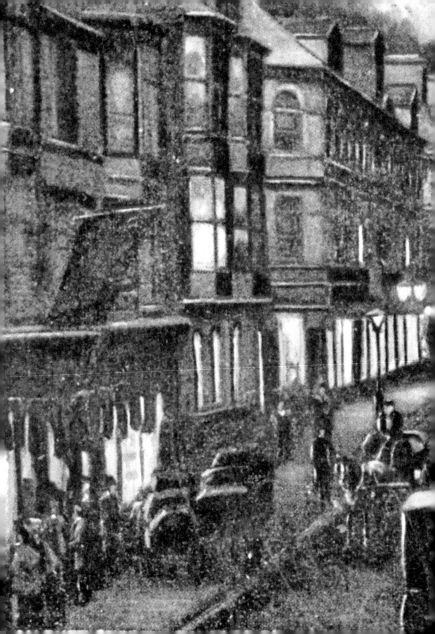

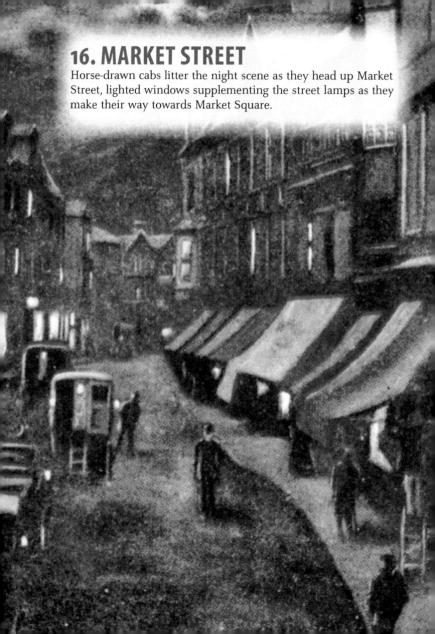

16. MARKET STREET

Horse-drawn cabs litter the night scene as they head up Market Street, lighted windows supplementing the street lamps as they make their way towards Market Square.

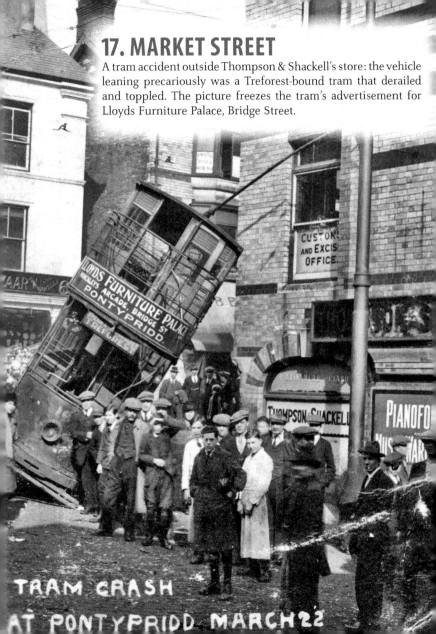

17. MARKET STREET

A tram accident outside Thompson & Shackell's store: the vehicle leaning precariously was a Treforest-bound tram that derailed and toppled. The picture freezes the tram's advertisement for Lloyds Furniture Palace, Bridge Street.

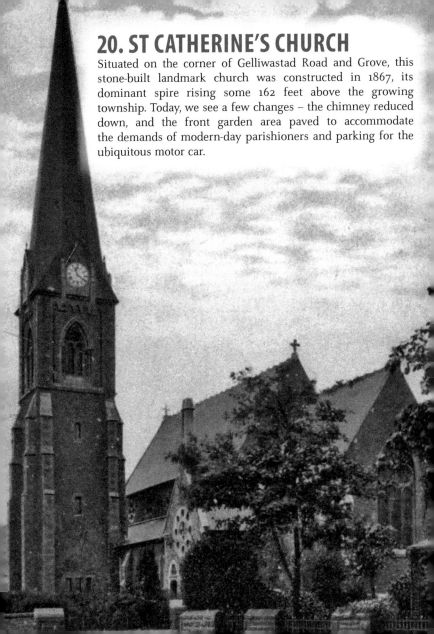

20. ST CATHERINE'S CHURCH

Situated on the corner of Gelliwastad Road and Grove, this stone-built landmark church was constructed in 1867, its dominant spire rising some 162 feet above the growing township. Today, we see a few changes – the chimney reduced down, and the front garden area paved to accommodate the demands of modern-day parishioners and parking for the ubiquitous motor car.

21. GELLIWASTAD ROAD

In the distinctive illustration, featuring a residential bias, the road is not as yet formally surfaced, and horse-drawn traffic is not a factor to concern the casual pedestrians. Today, the professional quarter has long occupied the original residences.

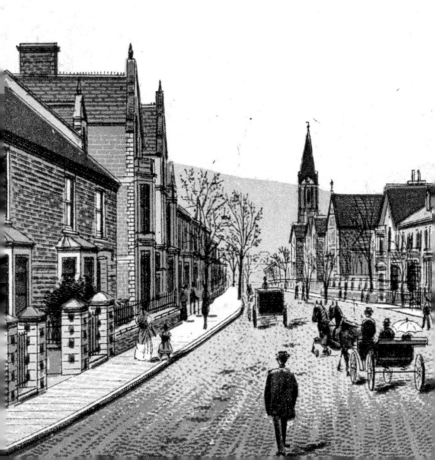

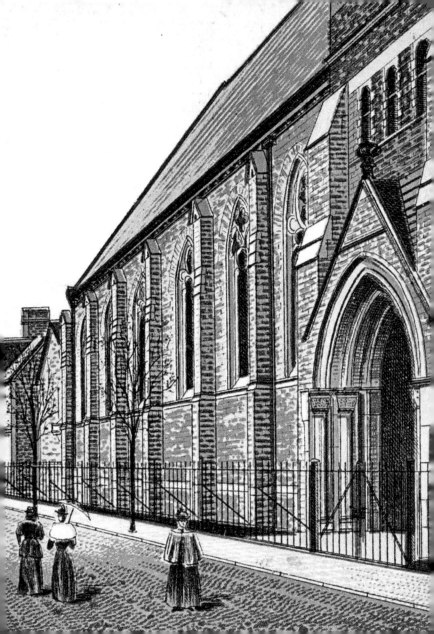

22. FREE LIBRARY

Completed in the 1890s, this innovative cultural initiative was successful in encouraging the burgeoning local population to read, featuring books in both Welsh and English. The elegant building features a turreted tower to break the orthodox roofline, and an interesting stone fresco of 'the bard' imposes his literary presence over the front portico.

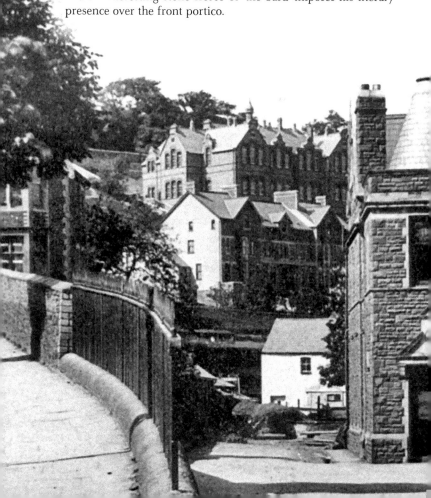

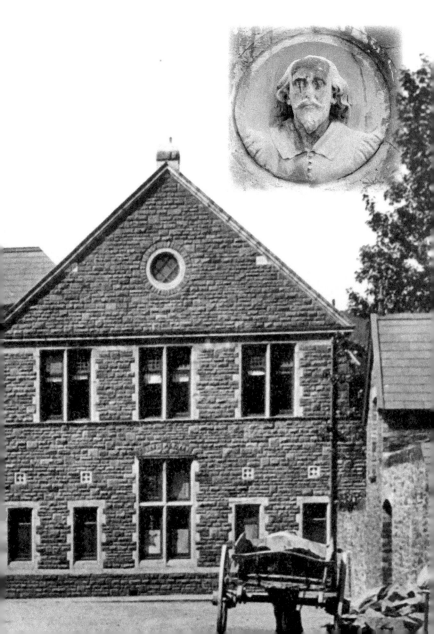

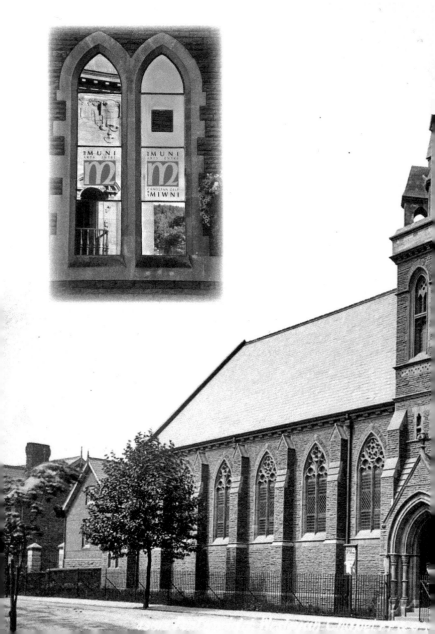

23. GELLIWASTAD ROAD

A significant early chapel founded by the Wesleyan branch of the 'non-conformist' Christian movement, this fine stone building represented an alternative place of worship to nearby St Catherine's. Today, this fine property serves the community as the Muni Arts Centre, offering a vigorous and popular venue for cultural arts and entertainment, including a cinema and theatre.

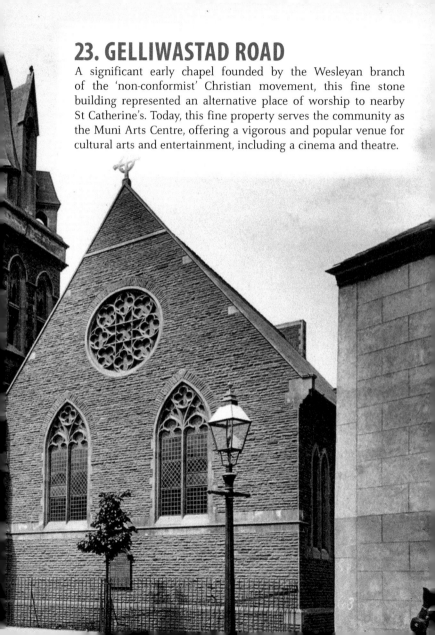

24. GRAIGWEN HILL

Soldiers of the Devon Regiment maintaining guard at Graigwen Hill were an unwelcome presence in the town. Pontypridd was the scene of the trials of thirteen of the miners involved in the Tonypandy Riots, though up to 10,000 marched in support. A convicted few served terms of two to six weeks at Cardiff prison. Soldiers stand on the steep, narrow, unmade road with an open drainage ditch during the long strike. Today, the widened road stands quiet, now providing access up to the residentially developed reaches of Graig Wen and Lan Wood.

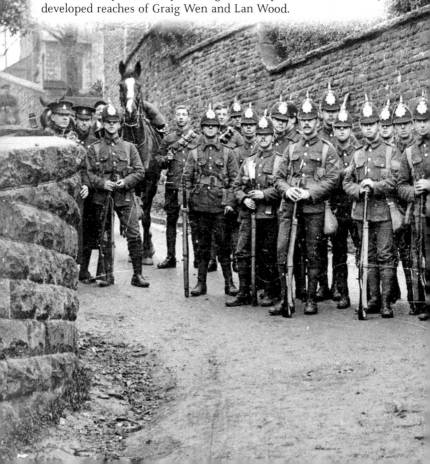

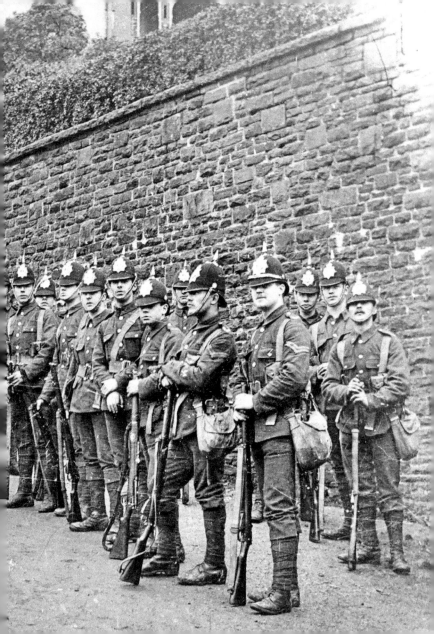

25. MILL STREET

Mill Street, long without the mill that gave it its name, is now a plethora of small premises serving the typical sole trader of goods and services, such as Jeremy & Edwards' 'High Class Provisions'. Today, new enterprises populate Mill Street's plurality of quaint fascias and hoardings.

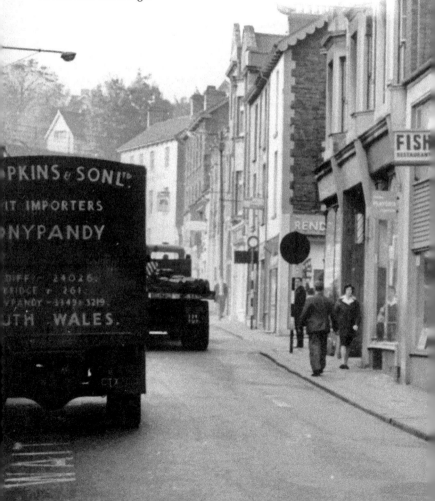

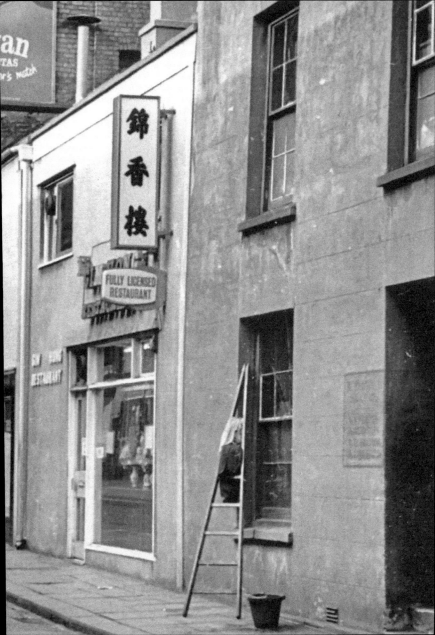

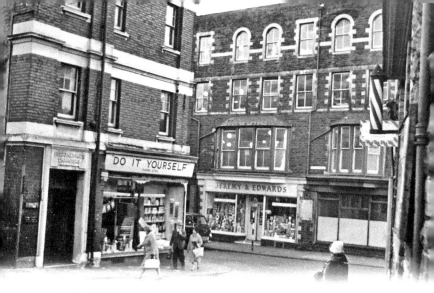

26. MILL STREET/CATHERINE STREET

The redevelopment of this very old area of the town has sacrificed much of Catherine Street, including the narrow portals of St Catherine's Chambers alongside the DIY store. The opposing shops, including the local barber's, have also disappeared. The artistically tiled pedestrian underpass now offers access to a totally different open area.

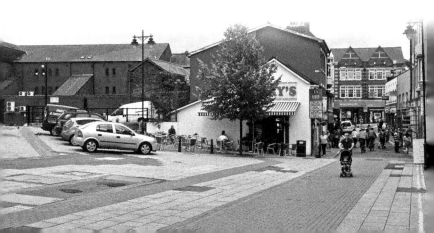

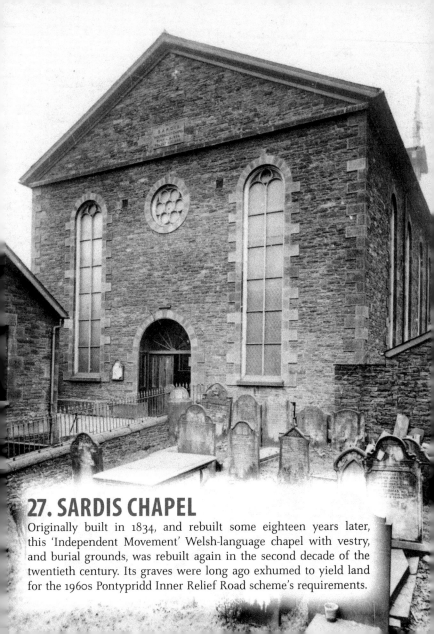

27. SARDIS CHAPEL

Originally built in 1834, and rebuilt some eighteen years later, this 'Independent Movement' Welsh-language chapel with vestry, and burial grounds, was rebuilt again in the second decade of the twentieth century. Its graves were long ago exhumed to yield land for the 1960s Pontypridd Inner Relief Road scheme's requirements.

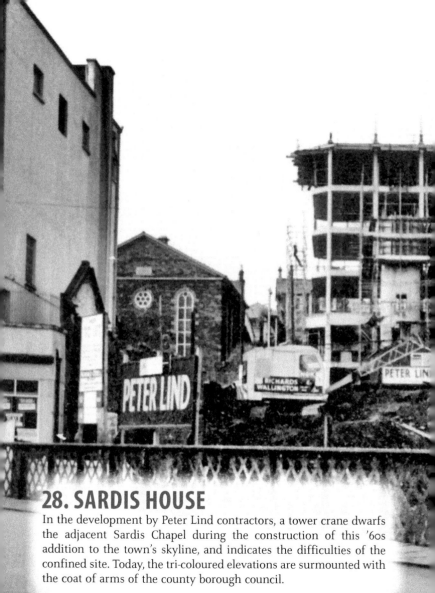

28. SARDIS HOUSE

In the development by Peter Lind contractors, a tower crane dwarfs the adjacent Sardis Chapel during the construction of this '60s addition to the town's skyline, and indicates the difficulties of the confined site. Today, the tri-coloured elevations are surmounted with the coat of arms of the county borough council.

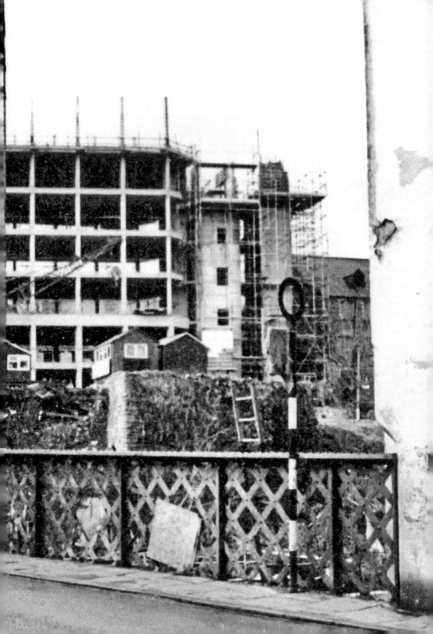

29. SARDIS PARK

One of South Wales' most iconic rugby clubs, Pontypridd RFC was first formed in 1876. The 1890/91 first team captain was Mr Ack Llewellin, who played with a hand-stitched leather ball. For many years, home ('amateur') fixtures were played at Taff Vale Park. The club has enjoyed a successful history, commanding a devoted following.

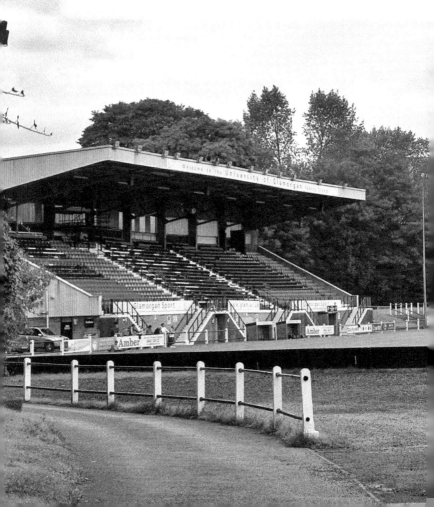

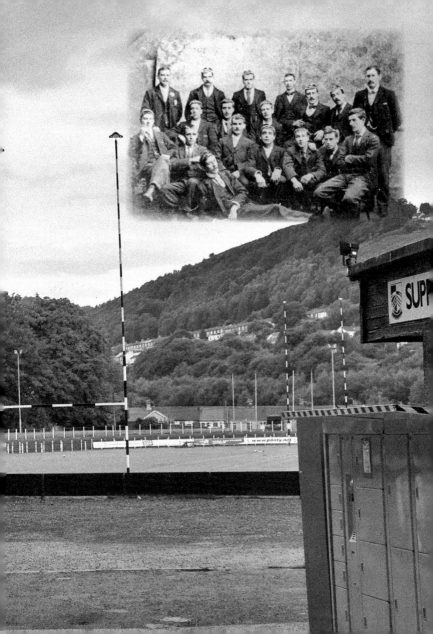

30. SARDIS BRIDGE

The total redevelopment of this corner for the approaches of the Inner Relief Road, showing the demolition of the old Sardis Bridge, police station and court. Creating a new profile to this old corner, tall, classical columns and the triangulations of symmetrical two-tiered gables compose the elegant elevations of the town's newest public building – Ty Pennant.

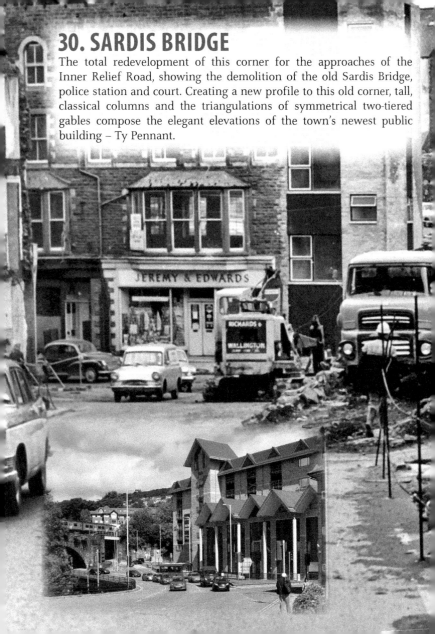

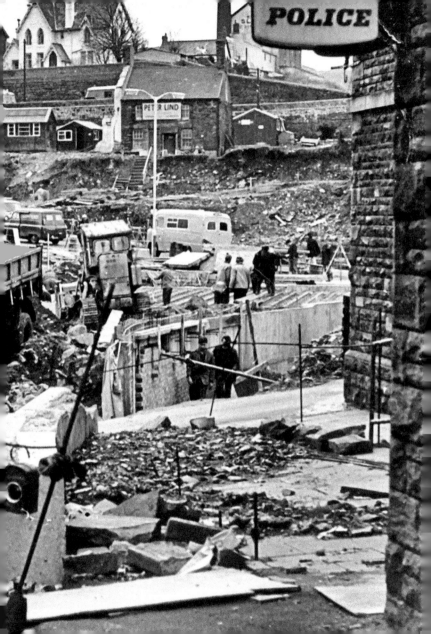

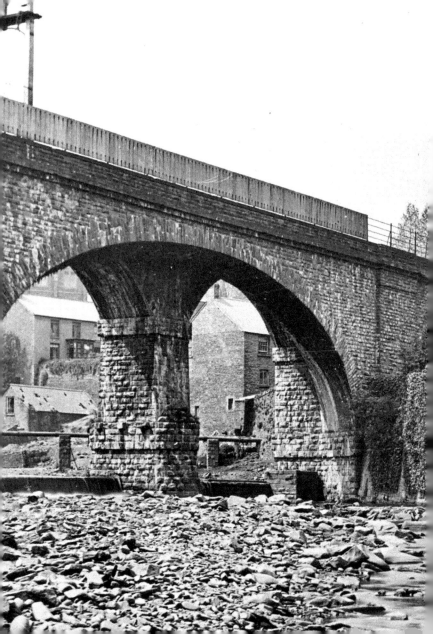

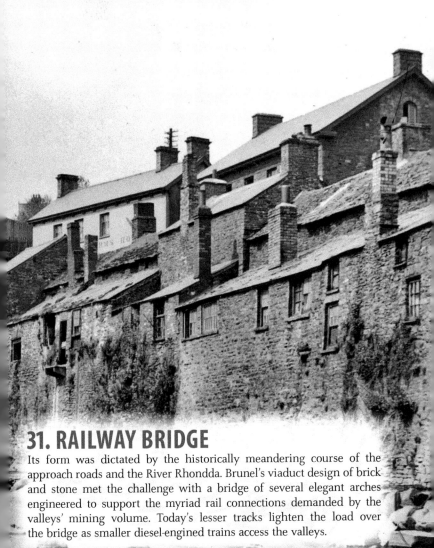

31. RAILWAY BRIDGE

Its form was dictated by the historically meandering course of the approach roads and the River Rhondda. Brunel's viaduct design of brick and stone met the challenge with a bridge of several elegant arches engineered to support the myriad rail connections demanded by the valleys' mining volume. Today's lesser tracks lighten the load over the bridge as smaller diesel-engined trains access the valleys.

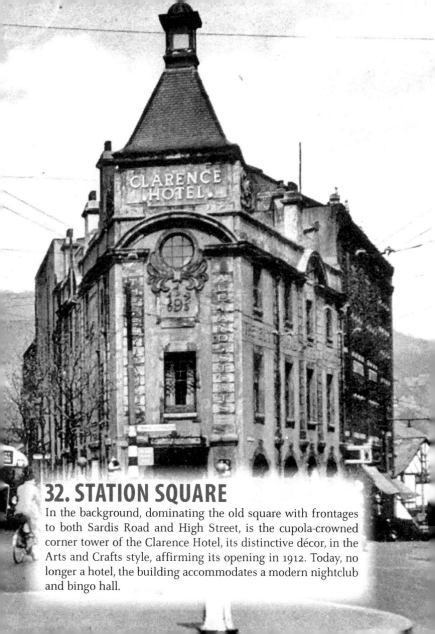

32. STATION SQUARE

In the background, dominating the old square with frontages to both Sardis Road and High Street, is the cupola-crowned corner tower of the Clarence Hotel, its distinctive décor, in the Arts and Crafts style, affirming its opening in 1912. Today, no longer a hotel, the building accommodates a modern nightclub and bingo hall.

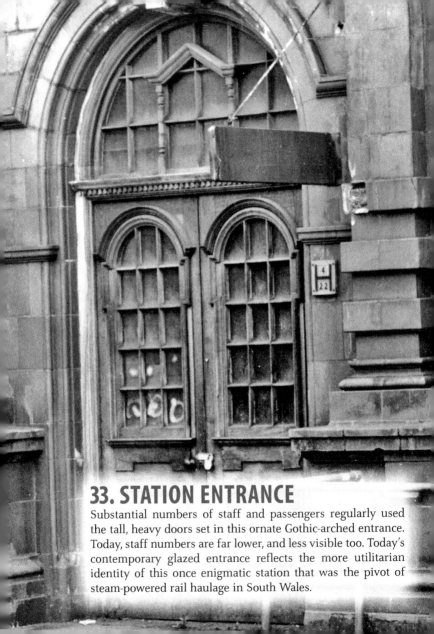

33. STATION ENTRANCE

Substantial numbers of staff and passengers regularly used the tall, heavy doors set in this ornate Gothic-arched entrance. Today, staff numbers are far lower, and less visible too. Today's contemporary glazed entrance reflects the more utilitarian identity of this once enigmatic station that was the pivot of steam-powered rail haulage in South Wales.

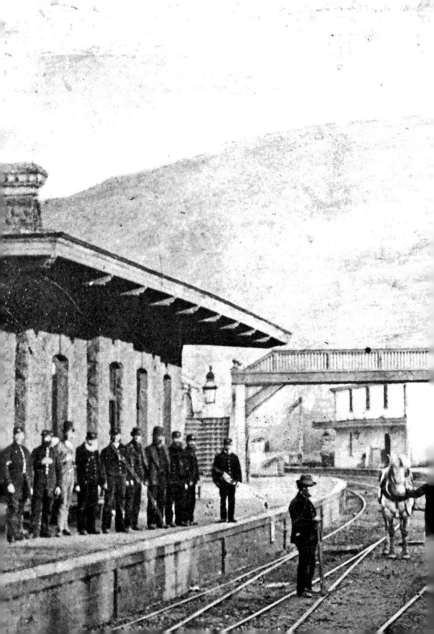

34. STATION PLATFORM

The concrete concourse was reputed to be the longest rail platform in the industrialised world, handling at its 1913 peak some 500 trains and 11,000 passengers a day. Alighting from the front compartment of a long Saturday 'special' felt like starting outside the town, such was the walk to the exit!

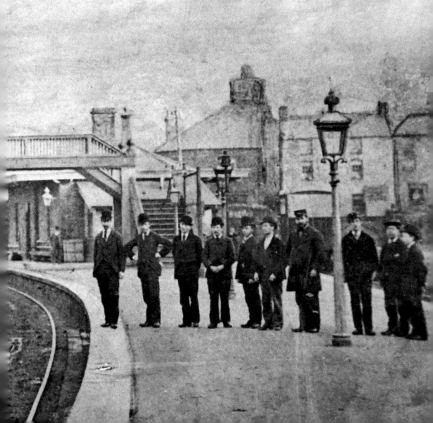

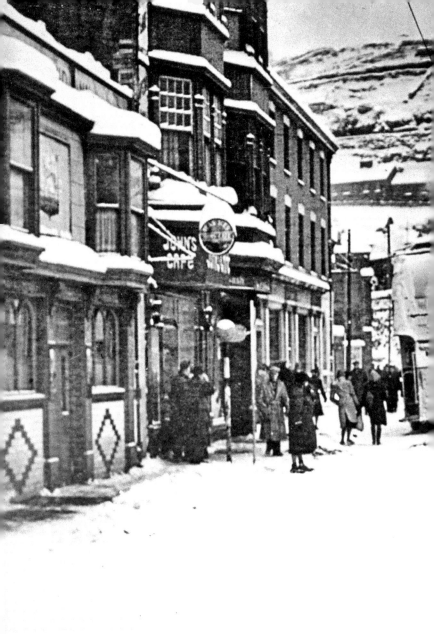

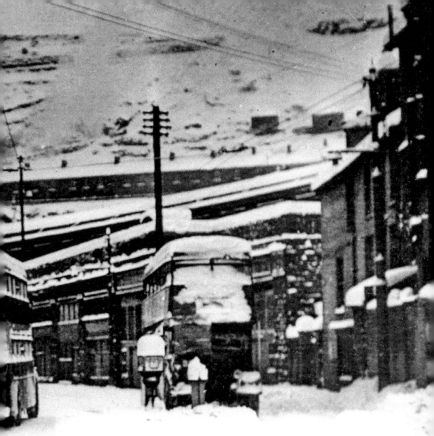

35. STATION SQUARE

A crisp, candescent covering coats the width of The Tumble as double-decker buses are stuck in the snow. A time perhaps for the crews to have a hot drink while awaiting the snowplough? John and Maria Orsi's café, in the left of the picture, was a welcome haven for all to enjoy the best of hot lunches, warming teas and coffees, or summer ice cream. Today, the spacious premises offer the cuisine of another nation – as the Oriental Buffet Chinese restaurant, open seven days a week.

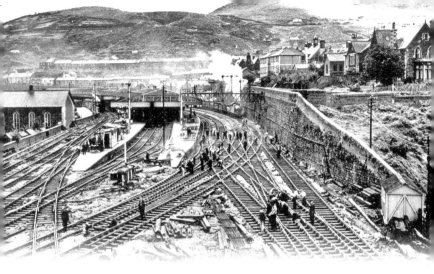

36. SPAGHETTI OF RAILS

The sweeping curves of metalled tracks had multiplied rapidly since the Taff Vale Railway Company's early (around 1840) initiative, recognising the town's strategic position to facilitate transport of iron, then coal, out of the three valleys to the docks of Cardiff, Penarth and Barry. Peak traffic of 1913 saw some 57 million tons of coal pass through Pontypridd. One-up, one-down tracks and a single passing loop are sufficient to meet today's different demands.

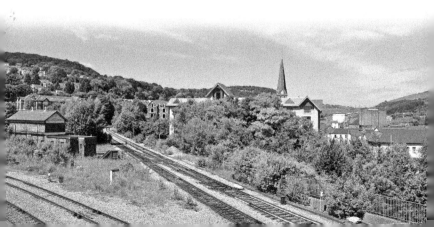

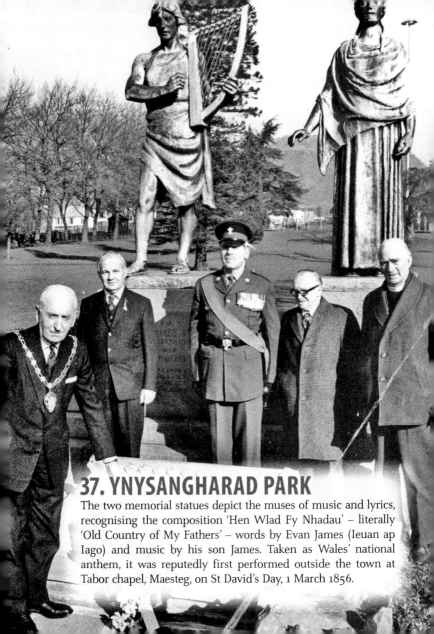

37. YNYSANGHARAD PARK

The two memorial statues depict the muses of music and lyrics, recognising the composition 'Hen Wlad Fy Nhadau' – literally 'Old Country of My Fathers' – words by Evan James (Ieuan ap Iago) and music by his son James. Taken as Wales' national anthem, it was reputedly first performed outside the town at Tabor chapel, Maesteg, on St David's Day, 1 March 1856.

38. YNYSANGHARAD PARK

Opened in 1923 as a living war memorial, this major town amenity was achieved by the raising of public subscriptions. It is a constant reminder of Pontypridd's previous prosperity, established during the town's pivotal contribution to the pioneer years of coal, iron, steel and tin production and transportation. Today, the Grade II listed park is still free for public use.

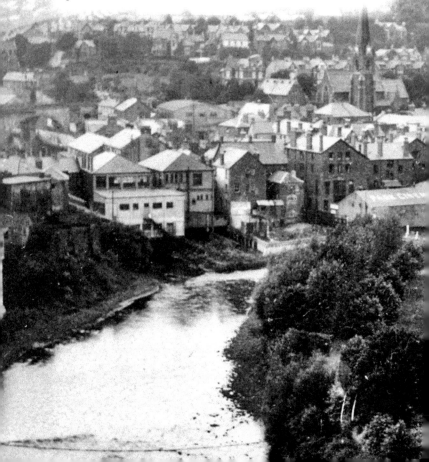

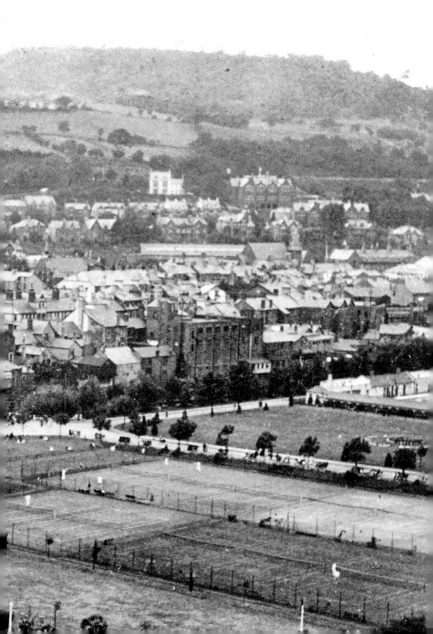

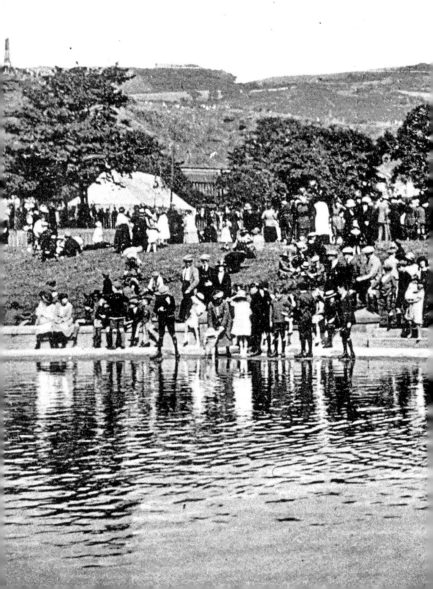

Paddling Pool. Ynysangharad Park, Pontypridd.

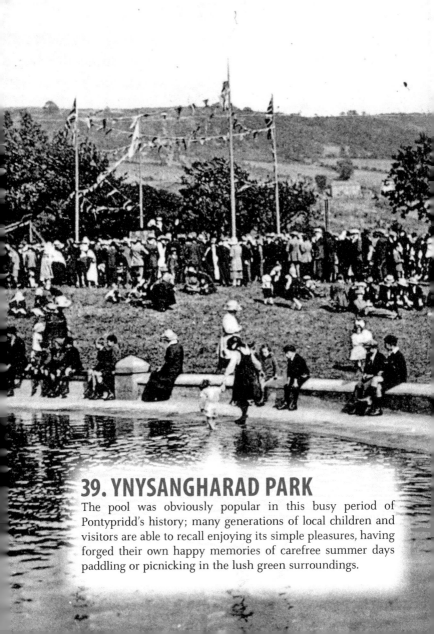

39. YNYSANGHARAD PARK

The pool was obviously popular in this busy period of Pontypridd's history; many generations of local children and visitors are able to recall enjoying its simple pleasures, having forged their own happy memories of carefree summer days paddling or picnicking in the lush green surroundings.

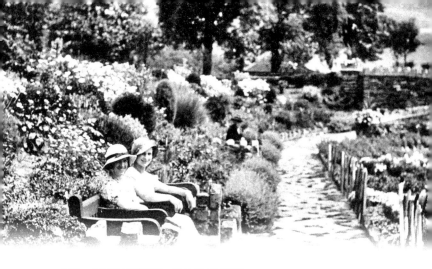

40. SUNKEN GARDEN

A stone's throw from the High Street's hustle and bustle, the formal tree-lined paths and planted avenues curtain the sunken garden from the busy world around. Today's garden still serves up those serene qualities, enhanced by the maturity of its approaches, remaining an enviable and relaxing location. The planted dram – a worthy, relevant memorial to lives lost in the once-dominant coal industry – was kindly donated to Pontypridd by 'Big Pit', Blaenafon.

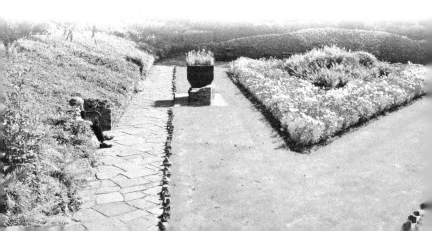

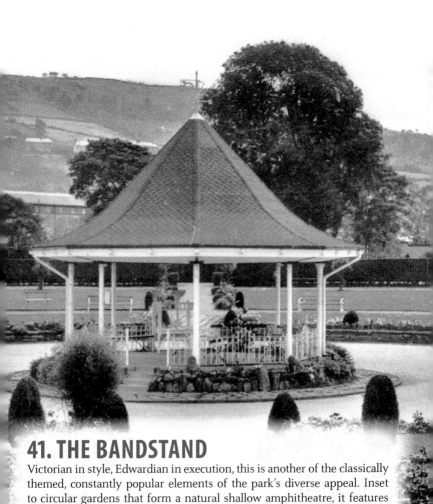

41. THE BANDSTAND

Victorian in style, Edwardian in execution, this is another of the classically themed, constantly popular elements of the park's diverse appeal. Inset to circular gardens that form a natural shallow amphitheatre, it features florally bordered symmetrical paths. In season, such colourful displays allow this picturesque, natural bowl to complement the proffered musical entertainment, or in quiet times to provide a relaxing refuge.

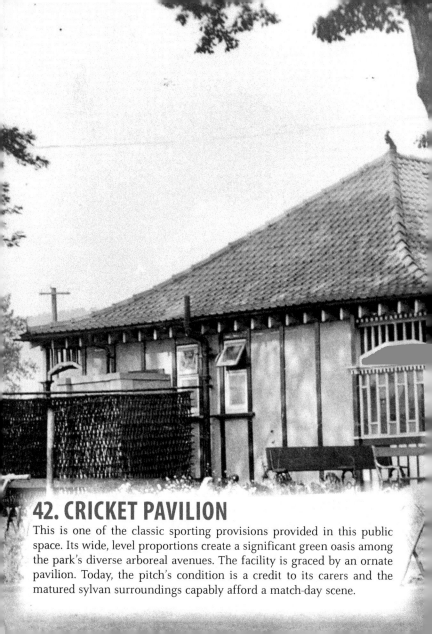

42. CRICKET PAVILION

This is one of the classic sporting provisions provided in this public space. Its wide, level proportions create a significant green oasis among the park's diverse arboreal avenues. The facility is graced by an ornate pavilion. Today, the pitch's condition is a credit to its carers and the matured sylvan surroundings capably afford a match-day scene.

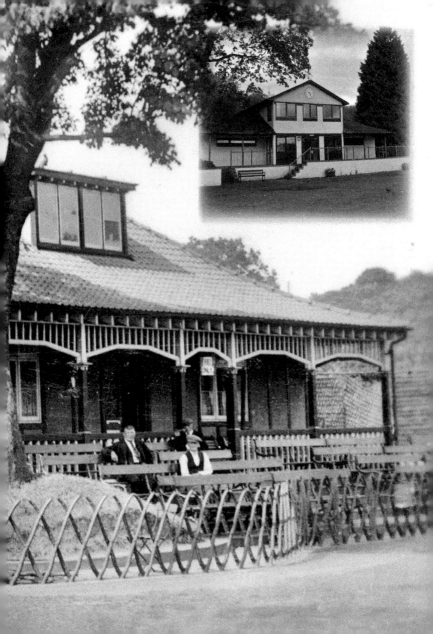

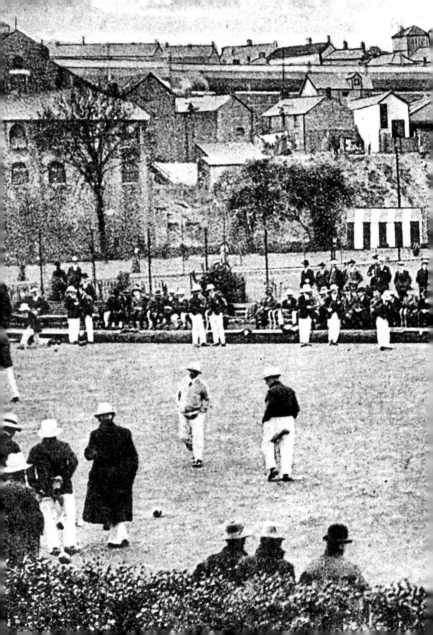

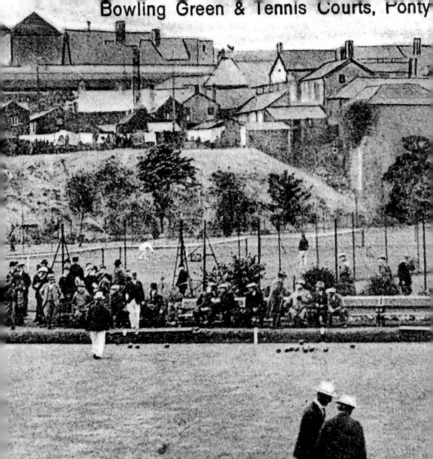

43. BOWLING GREEN

At this time, bowling was a pursuit for gentlemen and there was a competitive league. We see several ends in progress, encouraged by enthusiastic supporters. Today, two resting greens again reflect devoted attention and professionally applied maintenance. The greens continue to feature in Ynysangharad Park's well-used open-air sporting facilities.

44. TAFF BRIDGE

The bridge providing immediate access from Taff Street to the park's southern-corner attractions of bowls, tennis and cricket was just a short stroll from the workplaces of shops, offices and the market. Today, that bridge has been replaced by one of contemporary cantilevered design.

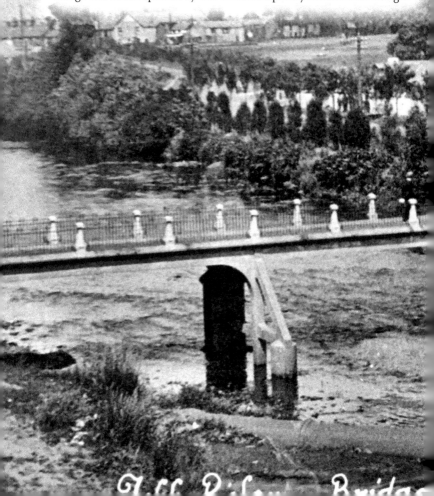

Taff Bridge

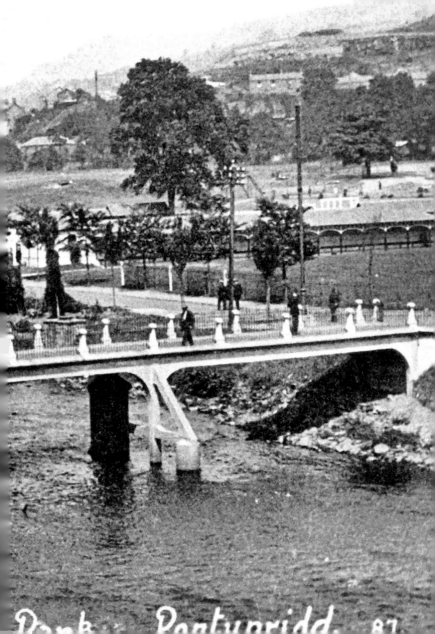

Park. Pontypridd. 87

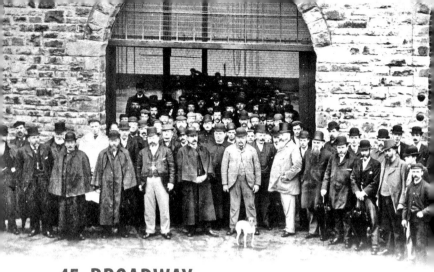

45. BROADWAY

Seemingly a jolly gathering, but – given the premises was a slaughterhouse at the time – hardly likely to have broadcast sweet tunes to this Broadway. Today, the same broad sweep of road carries the visitor into the south of the town, and the traffic is relieved by the A470's connection. Featuring a tree-lined formality, a residential recovery reflects in the townhouses' graceful bay windows, formerly part of the estate of Mrs Wickett and Mrs Thomas.

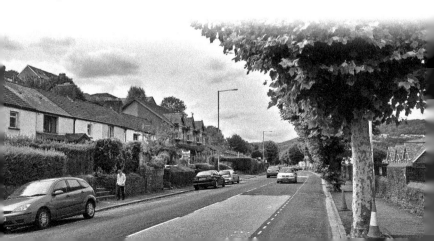

46. ST DUBRITIUS CHURCH

This church was dedicated to the Celtic saint Dubritius (his Latin name) around 1870. Dubritius founded a monastery at Henllan (Hentland) and taught many there, including St Samson. He was ordained as the first Bishop of Llandaff and Metropolitan Cambria in the sixth century. Several 'miracles' during his life and after his death are associated with him, including curing his grandfather of leprosy.

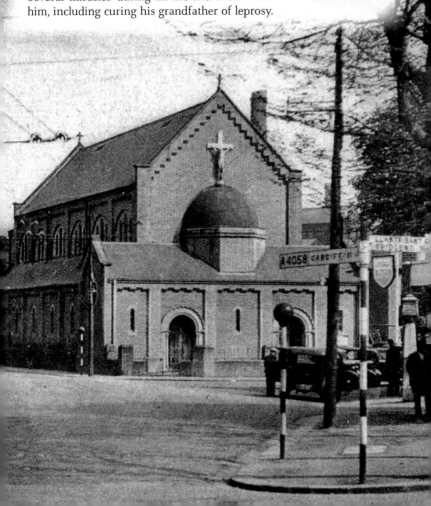

47. YNYSANGHARAD ROAD

The canal is shown with the nearby Brown Lennox Works buildings to the left of the picture. The Bunch of Grapes, built around 1800, is seen at the right of the picture – the temperance hall opposite soon followed its opening. A reputed visitor to enjoy a celebratory ale here was Isambard Kingdom Brunel, following a successful deal at nearby Brown Lennox in the early nineteenth century.

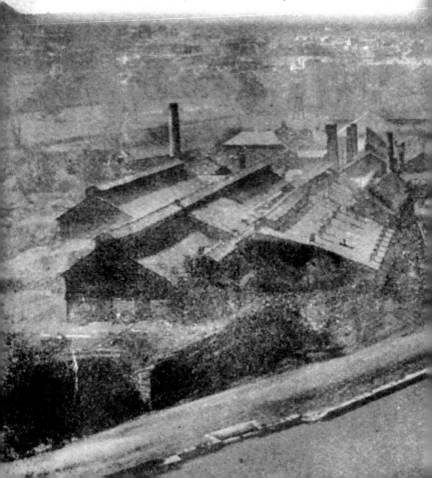

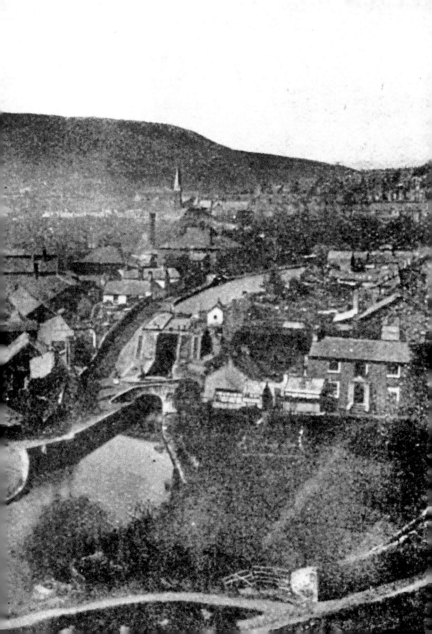

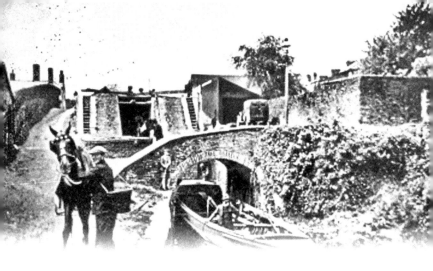

48. GLAMORGANSHIRE CANAL AND LOCKS

Reputedly, this is a Mr Bladon and his trusty horse working the towpath, the lockkeeper's cottage is on the right. The barge just clearing the stone bridge is heading towards Cardiff at this lower level. Building of the 25-mile canal, with fifty locks, commenced in 1790 at Merthyr and was fully open to Cardiff Docks by 1798. It was profitable for many years, though the railways encroached on its trade after 1841. In 1885, it was sold to the Marquess of Bute, who initiated improvements at Cardiff.

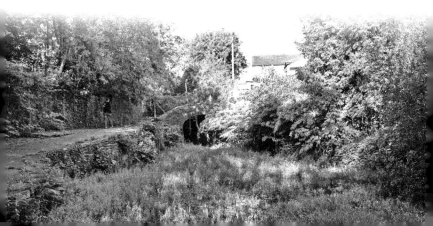

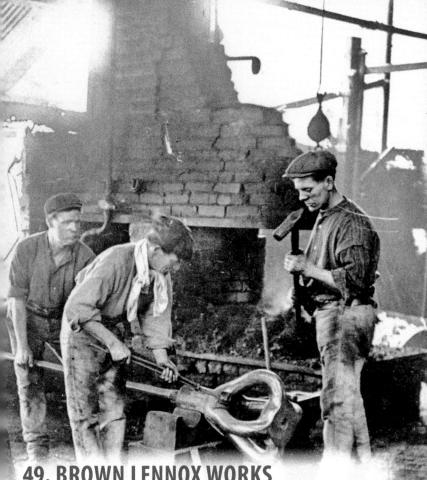

49. BROWN LENNOX WORKS

This iconic pioneer firm, formed by the two Samuels (cousins), was first called Newbridge Chain, Cable & Anchor, Ynysangharad, or 'Chainworkers Row'. Production commenced in 1818, following the success of Samuel Brown's 'stud-link' chain design, supplying Royal Navy and Merchant Navy ships, including Brunel's SS *Great Eastern*, up to 1916. Brown Lennox was a steady local employer in the 1950s and 1960s. A decade later, as demand for its traditional products fell away, the works finally closed after over 180 years in operation.

50. PONTYPRIDD COTTAGE HOSPITAL

The hospital was opened in 1911 by Clara Thomas of Llwynmadoc, Powys, who donated the princely sum of £500 at its inauguration. A Pontypridd street also carries the family place name. The refurbished and updated hospital today serves the community as a provision for patients requiring palliative care, and offering Macmillan Nursing services, physiotherapy and psychotherapy. It is also a day unit for the older mentally ill.

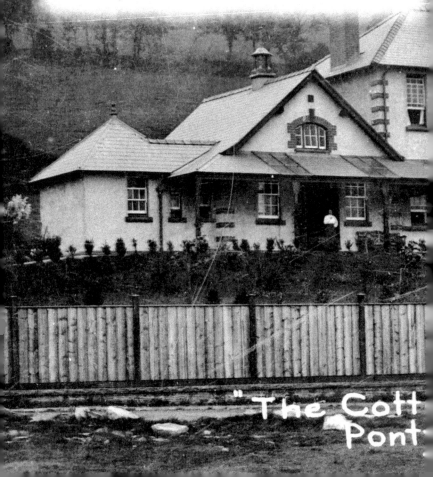

"The Cott
Pont.

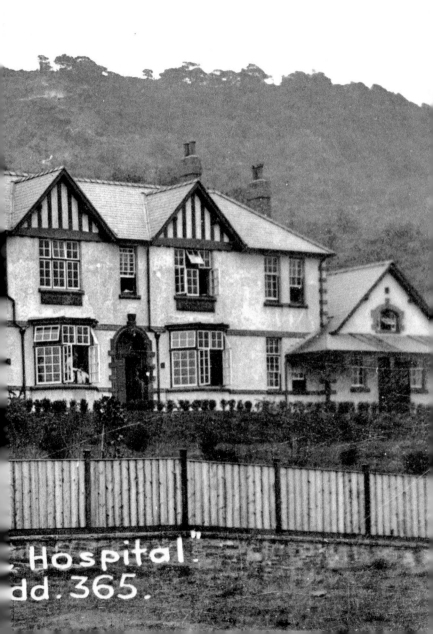

"Hospital".
dd. 365.

51. THE ROCKING STONE

Perched on the heights of Coedpenmaen Common, these distinctive weathered limestone obelisks (also known as Maen Chwyf and Y Garreg Siglo) form a Druidic circle set by the world-famous Dr William Price, pioneer of human cremation. The stones were added in the late 1800s to encompass the original, and famous, Logan or Rocking Stone. In 1842, he baptised his daughter on this stone, which apparently has a mass of around 10 tons, and is split across, so it lightly rocks. Today, it is still an interesting site for quiet contemplation. The modern township stretches across the topography below.

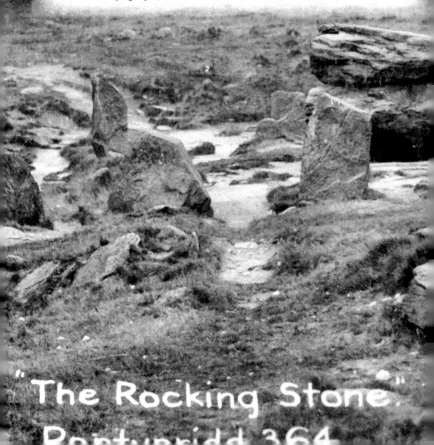

"The Rocking Stone"
Pontypridd 364

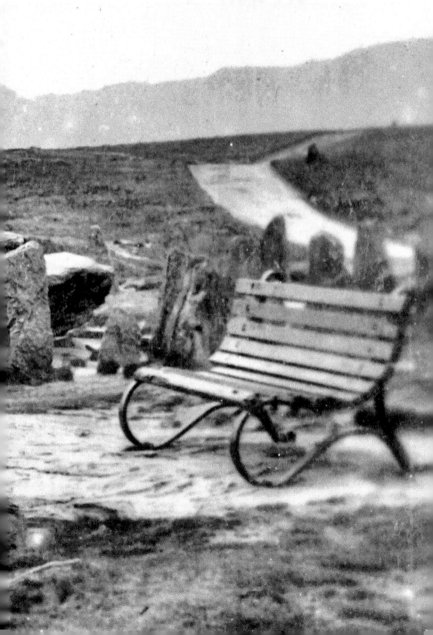

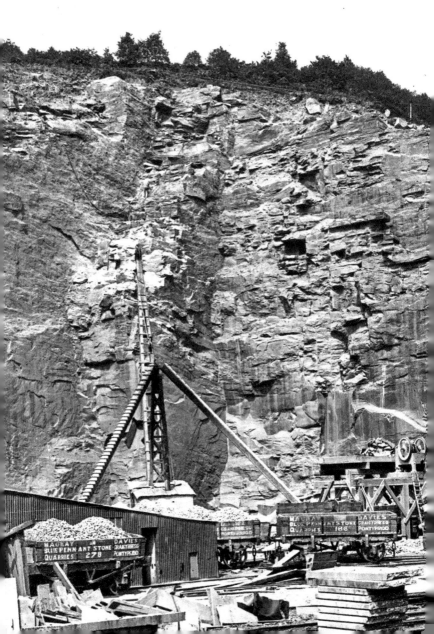

52. CRAIG-YR-HESG QUARRY

Early working of this edge-of-town quarry provided local building stone for the town's formative early expansion. It is evident today in the modern landmark building Ty Pennant at St Catherine's Corner. The quarry still yields stone in the twenty-first century and is currently owned and worked by Hanson Aggregates.

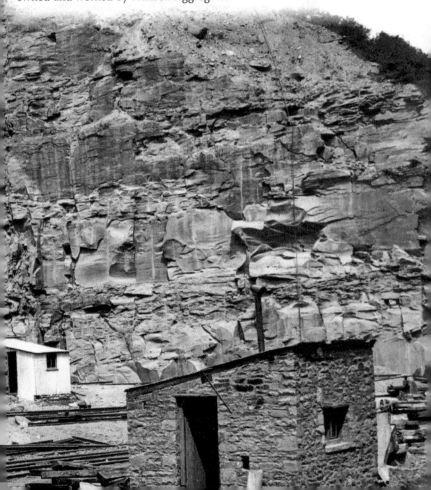

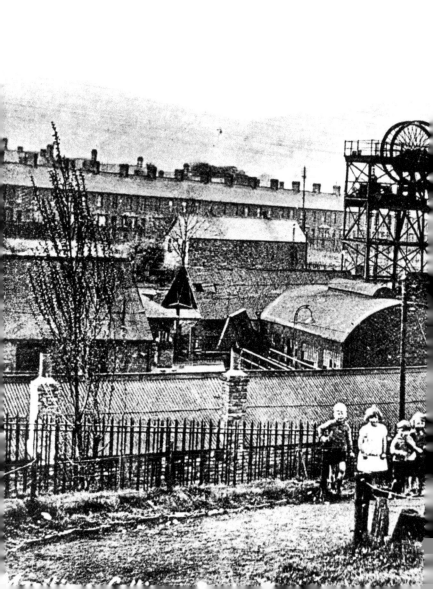

53. MARITIME COLLIERY

Boys and girls gather outside the Maritime colliery in the lee of the winding gear's stark outline. This pit is one of the early Great Western group sunk to access the coal seams of the geological 'Pontypridd anticline'. Today, clinging to the slopes of Mynydd Gelliwion, a floodlit sportsground and pavilion occupies a man-made plateau, achieved after reclamation works stabilised the spoil from these early mining initiatives.

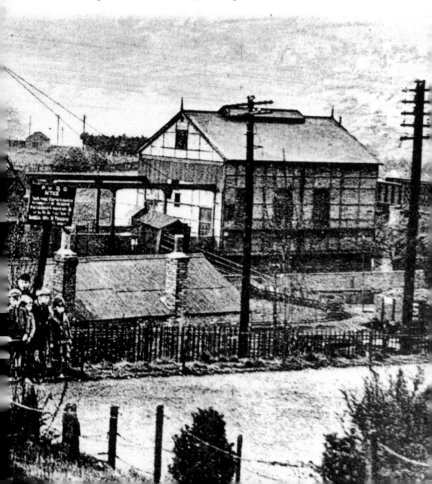

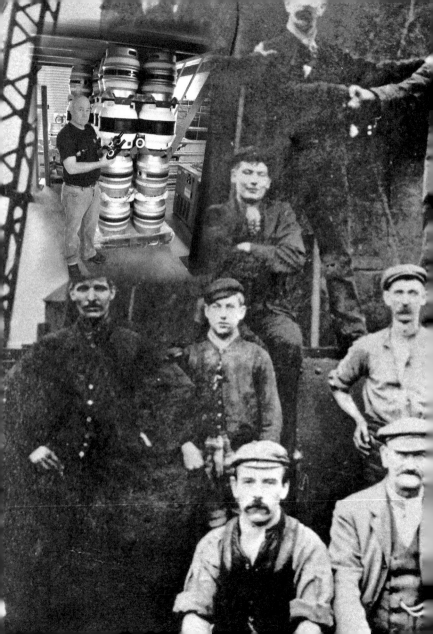

54. ALBION COLLIERY

This group illustrates the wide age range of those employed at that time in this hazardous industry. Today, part of this former colliery land, adjacent to the former line of the Glamorganshire Canal, is the site of the Albion Industrial Estate. Modern business enterprises, include the Otley Brewery – the recent venture of a local family of publicans whose founder started the business with the popular Otley Arms pub in Treforest. Brewer Charlie (inset) has already distinguished his company and town by winning a real-ale award for Otley's signature 'O' beer. Their distinctive black-and-white packaging and livery, incidentally, mirrors the colours of Ponty's venerable rugby club.

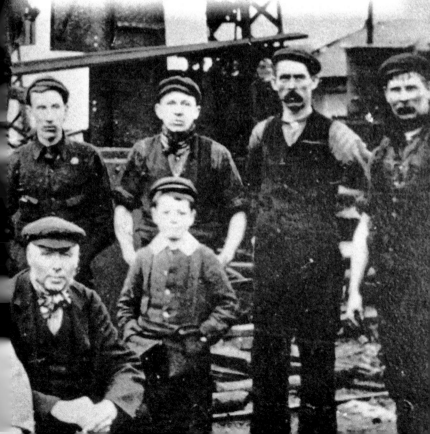

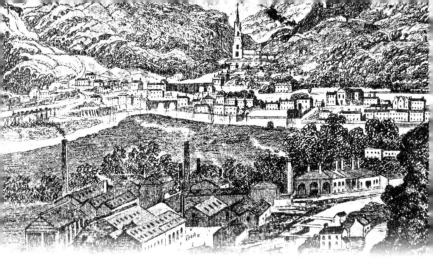

PONTYPRIDD TOWN

This early sketch of the town, *c.* 1870, illustrates its dominion at a time not long after the landmark spire of St Catherine's church first graced the town's skyline. The curve of the Taff is seen encompassing the riverside meadow, which was to become the people's war memorial park. In the foreground, the fledgling Newbridge Chain Works points its first tall chimneys at the sky alongside the canal locks.

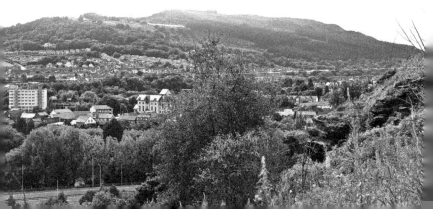